Rat Snakes

by Colleen Sexton

BELLWETHER MEDIA • MINNEAPOLIS, MN

BLASTOFF!
READERS
3

Note to Librarians, Teachers, and Parents:

Blastoff! Readers are carefully developed by literacy experts and combine standards-based content with developmentally appropriate text.

Level 1 provides the most support through repetition of high-frequency words, light text, predictable sentence patterns, and strong visual support.

Level 2 offers early readers a bit more challenge through varied simple sentences, increased text load, and less repetition of high-frequency words.

Level 3 advances early-fluent readers toward fluency through increased text and concept load, less reliance on visuals, longer sentences, and more literary language.

Level 4 builds reading stamina by providing more text per page, increased use of punctuation, greater variation in sentence patterns, and increasingly challenging vocabulary.

Level 5 encourages children to move from "learning to read" to "reading to learn" by providing even more text, varied writing styles, and less familiar topics.

Whichever book is right for your reader, Blastoff! Readers are the perfect books to build confidence and encourage a love of reading that will last a lifetime!

This edition first published in 2011 by Bellwether Media, Inc.

No part of this publication may be reproduced in whole or in part without written permission of the publisher. For information regarding permission, write to Bellwether Media, Inc., Attention: Permissions Department, 5357 Penn Avenue South, Minneapolis, MN 55419.

Library of Congress Cataloging-in-Publication Data

Sexton, Colleen A., 1967-
  Rat snakes / by Colleen Sexton.
    p. cm. – (Blastoff! readers: Snakes alive)
  Includes bibliographical references and index.
  Summary: "Simple text and full-color photography introduce beginning readers to rat snakes. Developed by literacy experts for students in kindergarten through third grade"–Provided by publisher.
  ISBN 978-1-60014-455-4 (hardcover : alk. paper)
  1. Rat snakes–Juvenile literature. I. Title.
  QL666.O636S49 2010
  597.96'2–dc22   2010000710

Text copyright © 2011 by Bellwether Media, Inc.
Printed in the United States of America, North Mankato, MN.

080110   1162

Contents

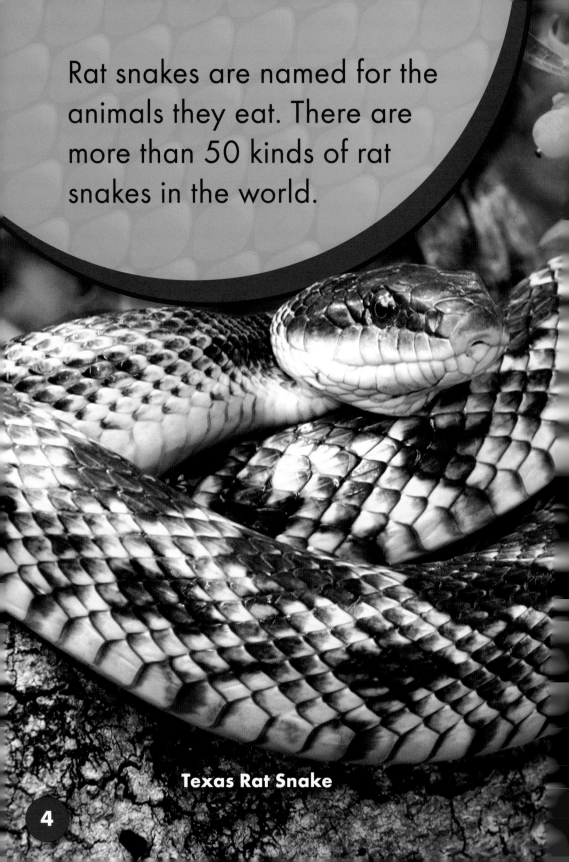

Rat snakes are named for the animals they eat. There are more than 50 kinds of rat snakes in the world.

Texas Rat Snake

Beauty
Rat Snake

Red-tailed Green
Rat Snake

Red
Rat Snake

Rat snakes come
in many sizes.
Most rat snakes
grow between 3
and 8 feet (1 and
2.5 meters) long.

Rat snakes come in many colors. Most are yellow, black, green, or gray. Some have stripes or spots.

Young rat snakes often have colors and markings that change as they grow.

Rat snakes have
wide, square heads.
Some have large eyes.
Their eyes let them see better
at night than most snakes.

Rat snakes have rounded backs and flat bellies. **Scales** cover and protect their bodies.

scutes

Large scales on their bellies called **scutes** help rat snakes climb trees.

The scutes grip on to rough bark.
Strong muscles pull on the scutes
and move the snake up the tree.

Rat snakes live in North America, South America, Europe, and Asia. They are plentiful in wooded areas and farmlands.

= areas where rat snakes live

Rat snakes use sight and smell to hunt. They stick out their forked tongues to pick up the scent of **prey**.

Rat snakes are known for hunting rats. They also eat mice, frogs, lizards, and other small prey.

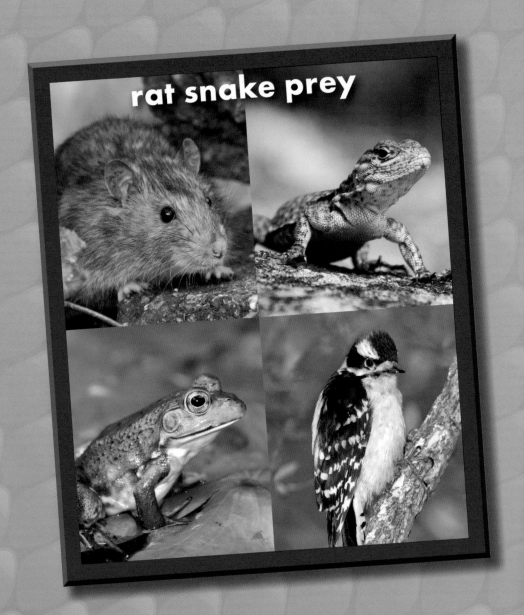

rat snake prey

Rat snakes **slither** into **burrows** to search for prey underground. They climb trees to catch birds. They even steal eggs from nests!

A rat snake grabs prey with its sharp, curved teeth. It wraps its strong body around the prey.

The rat snake squeezes its prey tighter and tighter. The prey cannot breathe and soon dies.

The rat snake stretches its jaws wide and swallows the prey whole!

Sometimes a rat snake must face a **predator**. The rat snake beats its tail against the ground to make a warning sound.

The rat snake also releases a foul-smelling liquid. The predator might think that the rat snake will taste bad.

The rat snake
hisses and raises
the front of its body
into an S-shape.
The predator takes
off before the rat
snake can **strike**!

Glossary

burrows—holes or tunnels in the ground made by animals

predator—an animal that hunts other animals for food

prey—animals that are hunted by other animals for food

scales—small plates of skin that cover and protect a snake's body

scutes—large scales on the belly of a snake that are attached to muscles; snakes use scutes to move from place to place.

slither—to slide

strike—to quickly throw the head and front part of the body at a predator or prey

To Learn More

AT THE LIBRARY

Gibbons, Gail. *Snakes*. New York, N.Y.: Holiday House, 2007.

Gunzi, Christiane. *The Best Book of Snakes*. New York, N.Y.: Kingfisher, 2003.

Thomson, Sarah L. *Amazing Snakes!* New York, N.Y.: HarperCollins, 2006.

ON THE WEB

Learning more about rat snakes is as easy as 1, 2, 3.

1. Go to www.factsurfer.com.

2. Enter "rat snakes" into the search box.

3. Click the "Surf" button and you will see a list of related Web sites.

With factsurfer.com, finding more information is just a click away.

Index

Property Of:
Millersburg
Elementary School

A.R. 2.?- 0.5 pt.